Somewhere to Go, Some Difference to Make

A Book of Observations

Mark D. Kimball

iUniverse, Inc.
Bloomington

Somewhere to Go, Some Difference to Make
A Book of Observations

iUniverse books may be ordered through booksellers or by contacting:

iUniverse
1663 Liberty Drive
Bloomington, IN 47403
www.iuniverse.com
1-800-Authors (1-800-288-4677)

ISBN: 978-1-4620-0117-0 (pbk)
ISBN: 978-1-4620-0118-7 (ebk)

Printed in the United States of America

iUniverse rev. date: 3/8/2011

For

GEORGANN and JASON

Founding Members of "The Doodlebug Express"

Author's Note

When I was thinking about writing a small book of observations, publishers asked questions like these:

For what audience did you write the book? When I explained that I essentially wrote it for me, they seemed puzzled. I think they were hoping for recipes from people who were on *Dancing with the Stars* or at least juicy gossip from someone in *Celebrity Rehab*.

What is your goal? Apparently, if you are not aiming for the bestseller list and a Pulitzer Prize, they doubt your commitment.

Actually, there are three pieces of good news for anyone who may risk a few minutes here:

The book is slim and is filled with short pieces that might give you food for thought or provide an idea or two you would want to share with a friend or loved one.

There will not be a quiz. Nothing in this little book will be on any final exam in any class.

If, as I sometimes do, you doze off, at least you will be getting some rest.

Contents

Part Two: Ten Things Your Children Should
            Know after Graduation

Part One: Reflections

Come along,

You brave men and daring women,

And we will go sailing with Ulysses!

Great work awaits,

As we ask the gods for guidance,

And fix our purpose

To serve goodness, truth, and beauty

In bold or quiet winds

And on still or foaming seas.

The Road Hole

Abraham Lincoln asked us to remember
  the better angels of our nature.
  On a smaller but still pertinent scale,
  true golfers know what he meant.

Life may have its challenges, sad ironies,
  and unforeseen disasters, often stemming
  from good intentions and bad timing.

But we keep going, moving forward
  with relentless optimism,
  celebrating the little victories along the way.

Nowhere is this truer than the 17th hole
  at St. Andrews, the home of golf.

After two encouraging critiques

from my caddy—

"There's a swing we won't be seeing

in the textbook," followed by

"Aye, laddie, we'll be sending the dogs

in after that one"—I was in front of

the famous bunker, surveying my sixth shot,

trying to figure out

how to stay out of the sand,

from where you would need a periscope

to see the pin,

and avoid hitting the road,

thus sending my ball to oblivion.

A perfect lob wedge

and one lovely putt later,

I had a great seven, a triple bogey

that still brings a smile to my face.

That is when I learned that

  golf is a microcosm:

It is success and failure, joy and sorrow,

  and proof that it is the struggle itself

  that ennobles and uplifts us.

Even when the result is not as good

  as we had hoped,

  it is also usually true

  that things could have been much worse.

And sooner or later,

  if we keep a clear head

  and a steady heart,

  we all have wonderful moments

  of pride and achievement:

On the course,

in the office,

at home,

everywhere.

The seven becomes a birdie.

You make that miraculous sale.

You get that promotion.

She says yes.

Your children become happy adults.

At the end of the day,

   the message of any carefully observed

   and honorably played

   round of golf

   is simply this:

Life is good,

Life is very good indeed.

Serendipity

In his bedroom

  there was a small table

  just right

  for a forty-four-month-old boy

  to color folksy pictures

  of his house,

  play with blocks,

  make things out of clay,

  have tea with his favorite stuffed bear,

  or, in this case,

  conduct emergency surgery.

The goldfish was clearly dead,

  yet he worked desperately,

  with almost flawless technique,

  to save his little friend,

turning the penknife

this way and that way,

looking for whatever

had made poor Harry

float

at the top of his bowl.

That was the day

we began to refer to him,

respectfully,

as Dr. Kimball,

a title he has had

confirmed

for many years

by the proper authorities,

who,

in their wisdom,

allow him to save

countless human Harrys and Harriets,

as we continue to tell

everyone who will listen

that we knew,

that he knew,

this is how it must be,

after he worked

alone in his room,

for almost two hours,

hoping to revive

his first pet

and his very first patient.

The Double Corona

Blue wisps of pleasure
  curl and drift and float
  slowly above my head
  on this balmy winter day,
As dark chocolate
  embraces the merlot,
  a friendly breeze allows the smoke
  to play a little longer in the air,
And I admire
  the graceful, light grey ash
  that I have so artfully nurtured
  to more than two inches,
Without once wondering
  what the world might be up to
  for nearly thirty
  sublimely solitary minutes.

Big Red

I saw him as a two-year-old.

Something said pay attention.

Something said just watch me.

Watch me put fear in their eyes

 And thunder in your heart.

Watch me run beyond the clock,

 Almost beyond imagination.

Watch me move like Man o' War

 With the rhythmic joy of Mozart.

That is what I heard

When I saw him for the first time.

And it all came true … every word of it.

Us

Sometimes stale coffee,

More often good wine,

I am yours and you are mine.

Close old windows

But open new doors,

You are mine and I am yours.

An unfinished poem

Improves line by line,

I am yours and you are mine,

And

I am yours and you are mine.

The Genesee Valley Hunt

Streams of mystical light,

as if announcing the arrival of angels,

poured through the branches.

Dew misted off the ground,

and steam lifted from the bodies

of the horses,

forming small clouds around their nostrils,

while they breathed nervously

in that perfect morning sun.

With anxious exhilaration,

we bounded from the woods

into the open air,

across a field of harvested corn,

hand galloping through time.

This is how it must have been

before telephones,

before radios

or even railroads,

when people rode with a purpose

well beyond pleasure.

I could hear the power

in their hooves

as dirt flew around us.

I could taste the sweaty excitement

as each rider

found his position

in what seemed like

a massive equine ballet.

And I could feel the supreme elation

and ultimate sense

of absolute freedom

in every person there.

It was wonderfully primeval,

exquisitely elegant,

profoundly dangerous,

and the most satisfying image

of nature

and our relation to it

that I have ever had.

I will never forget it.

Lorraine

Oh, to know her,

Before shadows took her breath away,

When love was yet unspoken,

And the world was still a place of wonder.

Oh, to aid her,

When pain embraced her heart,

Before sadness overflowed,

And hope still whispered in her ear.

Oh, to redeem her,

Before demons muted her prayers,

When anger became an ode,

And forgiveness was no longer possible.

Looking for Lincoln

Spurning myth and sentimental flood,

Through years of terrible fire and blood,

We went with songs of praise and sorrow,

Seeking yesterday for tomorrow,

Far beyond the marble and the bronze.

Struggling with the violence and gore,

In relentless search of something more,

We discovered him, when all was read,

Living his time but somehow ahead,

Still wise and right and stronger than stone.

A Winter Surprise

It should not have been there …

the season had passed.

The days were shorter, and the air was colder.

Even the rattlesnakes had gone to ground.

But there it was anyway …

a little desert daisy, alone in the rocks,

with three petals missing,

leaning into the late afternoon sun,

shaking against a brisk Nevada wind.

I stopped and stared for a long moment,

and found myself talking

to this strange small plant

 as if it were a friend or relative.

 "Good for you," I said. "Good for you."

Jack

If you have ever had a dog and lost him, you know how we feel about Jack.

Named for JFK, Jack Kerouac, the great boxer Jack Dempsey, and my younger brother John, he was truly a rascal: a happy, muscular, energetic, and mischievous little Jack Russell terrier.

He could jump as high as any carrot could be thrown, but he continually fell short when the local blackbirds took flight as he chased them away.

He did a great imitation of James Cagney if any dirty rat ventured into his territory … which was clearly and professionally marked on a regular basis.

UPS trucks were allowed but were charged a two-bark toll … and the drivers knew, if they would walk softly and throw a small stick, they would have a friend forever.

As a guest in our dining room, he never pawed or whined, just waited patiently until you inevitably had one bite less of your steak.

While he could play at length in the snow, he really appreciated the warmth of a fire in the evening, especially if someone would massage lightly behind his ears.

Toward the end, he was still regarded as The Man in our neighborhood, walking on his leash with such an air of self-confidence that other dogs felt privileged to greet him.

He is gone now, and we miss him, almost as if a member of the family had passed away. If you have ever had a dog and lost him, you know exactly how we feel.

The Postgame Interview

Reporter: Coach, you haven't defeated a top twenty-five team in almost fifteen years. Talk about the significance of this game, especially now that your record has improved to 5-4.

Coach: (Imagine all caps if the coach is from a BCS conference in the Midwest or the South.)

Well, I'm just thrilled for the kids. Give all the credit to my coaches, the players, and the best fans in the country. This is a great day for the university and the entire state.

We never looked ahead. We never took anything for granted. We knew we would have to man up and bring it to them.

We took it one day at a time in practice and one play at a time during the game.

We never gave up. We always believed we could win, that we would win.

You know, this is what football is all about. This is what America is all about. It makes all the sacrifices worthwhile: all those two-a-days, all those late night film sessions, all those long recruiting trips.

Our young quarterback was outstanding. He managed the game perfectly. The two interceptions and the fumble weren't his fault. When the going got rough in the second half, he really got going. He is just a great kid, a great student, and a great American. During the off season, he works for the Saint Peter Foundation. He is not only our best chance for a Heisman trophy, but also our best hope for world peace.

I think if the voters really pay attention, you'll see us right up there with a shot at the national title. Week in and week out, we play the toughest schedule in the toughest conference. It is an amazing grind that many other teams never face. And our non-conference games include some of the strongest I-AA teams from the Shady Tree Conference.

There may be six undefeated teams ahead of us, but most of them are from lesser leagues on the West Coast or the Mountain Whatever.

We have a great tradition, and we can compete with anybody, anywhere, anytime, and we are looking forward to strapping on our pads next week and showing everyone that we are better than those pesky, stalwart, and often heroic Purple Mosquitoes.

Billy, Doc, and Wyatt

More than villains,

Less than heroes,

We see them …

In the mists of the morning air,

And the dust that blows across the prairie.

More than outlaws,

Less than victims,

We feel them …

In the endless desert heat,

And the howls of coyotes in the night.

More than a lie,

Less than the truth,

We need them …

In the West we still yearn for,

Still open, still sprawling, still beckoning

To adventure, danger, progress, hope, and glory.

Today

Tomorrow, I will do all my work,
  no call unanswered,
  no complaint unheard,
  no issue unresolved.
But not today.
Today, I choose you.

Sitting here together,
  doing nothing or anything
  is the only something
  on my mind.

Holding your hand
  or kissing your cheek
  is the only business
  I will conduct …

Unless you want to walk

  barefoot on the beach,

  or I make your favorite

  omelet for brunch,

  or wash your hair,

  color your nails,

  run your bath

  and wash your back,

  or you have some other wish

  that becomes my command.

Tomorrow, I will do all my work,

  on time,

  all the time.

But not today.

Today, I choose you.

Amelia

"No, thank you," she said,

with bold, bright eyes

when I offered to push her chair into the dining room.

"I'm just getting my muscles ready."

All ninety pounds of her

gave me a broad smile,

and then she grabbed the big black wheels and rolled away.

Watching her,

I wondered what lucky man

might have met her

fifty years or so ago

and been smart enough to fall in love forever.

To Thomas Jefferson

You were often wrong
 And just as often slow,
But history must be fair, Tom,
 And I forgave you long ago.

Some only hear the darker words
 And never let them go,
But I have heard the music, Tom,
 And I forgave you long ago.

I hope they find the notes
 And someday feel the flow,
But you changed the world forever, Tom,
 And I forgave, and learned to love you,
 Long ago.

When Did I Become Irrelevant?

It wasn't when I announced,

  two years in advance,

  that I would retire.

In fact, for most of that time,

  I felt more than appreciated.

  I knew I would be missed,

  even if only by some,

  and only for a little while.

It wasn't when we first moved to Nevada.

  For several months,

  we were just … well … free …

  free to go here, see this, do that,

  and even spend within reason,

without any sense

that anyone would notice

or frown

or gossip

or second guess in any way.

Isn't it actually now,

  right now,

  that we are settled

  with no ambitious plans

  beyond dinner,

  that the truth is clear:

Not only will no one notice,

  but essentially, no one will care.

No one will say,

  here he comes,

  he'll know what to do,

  or even,

  we better do our homework,

  you know how thorough

  he likes us to be,

  or even,

  with disapproval,

  yeah, the old tyrant,

  he's usually wrong anyway,

  why should this time

  be any different?

At least then

  your existence is real,

  you count for something

  in the world,

  you actually matter.

Instead,

tomorrow looking very much like today,

I am quietly at home

with a wisely forbearing woman,

who graciously hands me

a glass of cabernet,

as I comment again

on the growth of the grass

and the progress of the mimosa tree.

Another Thing That Only Happens to Me

There I was,
    drying my hands in a restroom at Burger King,
    on one of those forced air machines
    that takes five minutes to work …
While, in a nearby stall,
    a man was struggling heroically
    in one of the epic battles
    in the history
    of indoor plumbing,
    leaving me on sensory overload,
    torn between repulsion and admiration.
In the end,
    the lethargic blower won out,
    and I was finally forced
    to order a burger and diet cola to go,
    with dripping hands
    and a soggy five-dollar bill.

For David

Listen, my friend,

I know it isn't fair,

and you didn't do anything wrong.

You shouldn't be lying here

wondering what happened,

how you went

from a little cough

to the lights and siren

of the emergency crew.

You couldn't foresee

a ventilator,

the waves of amnesia,

the surrealistic visions,

those puffy hands, bleeding lips,

and countless liquid meals.

But here you are

with nothing to do

but give in or get better,

which is more your decision than you think.

Remember what the doctor said

and the nurse repeated,

and what we will recite every hour:

The only way out of here

is to walk out,

all the way out,

without help,

without the chair,

the cane,

the crutches,

or anything else.

Let's begin today.

It will be awkward,

even painful, at first,

but it only takes one step

to start,

and then one more,

and then two more, and five more,

and twelve more,

until there are no more …

And we all end up at your house,

just in time

for my famous corned beef hash,

an inviting amber ale,

and the first big night

of the college football season.

Gettysburg

If I were there with a choice

  not based on blood or sand,

  I would have been in blue,

  standing for the flag

  and for the Union,

  with the battle cry of freedom

  on my lips.

Like continental plates shifting

  beneath the earth,

  a reckoning had come upon us,

  and we would fiercely defend our hill,

  in that ghastly death-soaked valley,

  not for honor or the glory,

  but to try to put things right.

I would have cheered

   to see them turning back,

   proud of our prevailing there,

   grateful for the strength

   to do what had to be done,

   and sadly accepting

   that it had to be done at all.

And I would have gone weeping,

   down the days

   and down the nights,

   for the brave lost boys

   of Bobby Lee …

For the farmers and the clerks

    and the fathers and the sons

    who would always be coming,

    with calm resolve,

    through the thick black smoke

    into cannons they could not see.

Weeping for the families

    losing one by one

    their doomed and dying men,

    falling for the final time

    in a northern field of wheat,

    or lying twisted, hard, and cold

    in the unforgiving rocks

    along the ridge.

If ever safely home,

  though darker memories

  may never fade,

  I would tell and tell again,

  with gravely honest affection,

  how we were right and why,

  in our massive summer struggle

  with those grand and gallant

  soldiers of the South.

Up with ABBA

Go ahead.

Enjoy *Mama Mia.*

Let the silly story

  stick in your brain

  like old bubble gum.

Let the dreary dialogue

  roll and bounce

  through your ears

  until it finally fades away.

And then …

Let that miraculous music,

  that irresistibly enthusiastic rhythm,

  make you sing and dance

  until the only feeling left

  is the most genuine sense of joy,

  because you are

  or know someone who is

  a truly enchanting,

  remarkable,

  and permanently delightful

  dancing queen.

Harry Potter

Yin	Yang
Mumbo Jumbo	Holy Hogwarts
Can't Say Why	Don't Care Why
Mumbo Jumbo	Holy Hogwarts
Pie In The Sky	Soar Through The Sky
Mumbo Jumbo	Holy Hogwarts
No One Knows	Everyone Knows
Mumbo Jumbo	Holy Hogwarts
And On It Goes	AND ON IT GOES

Pleasant Valley Manor

We did not put them there today.

she said,

although it was probably not harmful

or oppressive,

or even unpleasant,

there must be,

at least for her parents,

at least for now,

something more than

three easy meals,

an afternoon sing-a-long,

the tuesday shuttle to a casino

and a weekly visit to walmart.

i thought,

but did not say,

it was somewhere i could never go,

knowing full well i might,

and was,

despite the necessary

and professional care,

one of those places

that is painfully polite,

where everything is a pretty pale blue

and someone plays the piano

until you die.

And so I agreed.

We did not put them there today.

Come to Me

Come to me.

Come slowly,

  not because I am older now,

  but because that has always been the better way.

Come with small favors,

  letting their memory linger

  in my mind,

  through difficult days and long, lonely nights.

Come with your graceful hands

  and generous heart,

  and then,

  when we are quietly complete,

  whisper me softly to sleep once again.

Miss Roberts Saves the Day

"What's wrong?" she asked gently to the weeping child.

"I can't do this homework."

"Why not, sweetheart?"

"I can't spell good enough to write what I saw in the park," he said, sobbing softly.

"Well. I know you can draw. Why don't you try that?"

"But that isn't what you asked us …"

"That's all right, dear, just draw me a nice picture," she said, as she touched his shoulder. "We will keep working on your spelling."

Twenty-five years later, an artist displays on a central wall of his first major exhibition the immature but promising folk art impression of his family picnic with the A+ from Miss Roberts circled in red.

An Oldie but Goodie

Take a ride with me,

I suggest to my neighbor's query.

Open the generous door

and slide straight in

with no painful pressure

on your hips or on your knees.

Sit in that broad front seat.

Stretch your legs out.

Be comfortable.

Pull down your own armrest.

Put your briefcase next to you,

where my wife puts her shopping bag,

newspaper, magazine, coupons and purse,

without invading my space at all.

Look at the dials:

easy white during the day,

calmingly green in the dark.

Notice the speed smiling up at you

in bright three inch numbers.

And, by all means, check the computer

along the highway to Vegas.

Yes, it really says twenty-seven.

I'm sure you are right, though.

They will no longer be offering

this unfortunate dinosaur to an aging public,

because, after all, times do change,

and new is always more appealing.

But this is also true:

they won't get the keys to my Mercury Marquis,

or the keys of thousands of other drivers

on fixed incomes,

for many years and millions of miles,

as we continue to glide across America

in safe and golden comfort.

America, Oh, America

America, Oh, America,

I sing your cherished song

in the sacred key of hope

that lights the world …

I see your scars,

but I sing your deep down beauty,

bluer than your spacious skies,

more golden than the fields

that please the eye …

I know your sins,

yet I sing an endless season of dreams

with ancient and familiar words

that stir the soul:

freedom,

opportunity … equality,

enterprise … endurance,

fairness … generosity,

honor,

innovation and tradition …

I sing out loud,

as a son sings proudly

who loves his aging and imperfect mother,

a full throated and grateful song

of glory long ago and far ahead,

of the best a wounded world has known

or is ever likely to know,

America, Oh, my America.

Grammy Has a Birthday

Play one more tune for us, Mabel,

Come sing and take a bow,

And we'll laugh together, Mabel,

To enjoy the here and now.

Let's find your golden necklace, Mabel,

And the earrings you love to wear,

And we'll dress you gaily, Mabel,

With bright ribbons in your hair.

You may rest tomorrow, Mabel,

And sleep both noon and night,

But we'll dance today, sweet Mabel,

While we can still hold you tight.

Death Valley

Look closely.

As the sun moves slowly

Over the drifting mounds,

Unlimited shades of grey,

Tan, black, and brown

Shiver and shift

Through the changing light of day.

The hills perform at sunset,

As if they were flowers

In an elegant English garden,

Pink blossoming to orange,

Exploding to red,

Blazing to purple,

Gleaming into a hue so haunting

That we simply stare in wonder.

And then,

Almost without warning,

Colors fade,

And shadows fall,

As a crisply cool

And sudden stillness

Comes to the evening desert air.

If you have not come to our valley,

You should.

You will love it,

If you look closely.

Cody Powell and Carson Wyatt

I have two grandsons.

Both are named for western legends.

They are fine boys with upstanding parents. I'm sure they are destined for good schools and will have outstanding careers in something or other.

But right now, they are just boys, which means they can do things their mom and dad can't even think about.

No, the only one who can be like them is me … because I'm the grandpa … and I'm supposed to be a little off.

We are the opposite ends of the rainbow: totally different and exactly alike.

Ask yourself this:

Would it be okay if your pants fell down at the supermarket?

Can you take a nap anytime you feel like it?

What happens if you tell the truth to everyone you know?

Would you go to work in plaid pants, a striped shirt, argyle socks, and pink sneakers?

In a restaurant, how much of the burrito is on your shirt?

Do you completely undress on your way to the bathroom?

How many really funky hats do you own? Which of them do you wear to church?

If you can't remember why you opened the refrigerator door, do you just laugh and ask Mom why you went there in the first place?

We all collect things. How many toads do you have?

Have you climbed into the sink this week and laughed so hard you peed your pants?

Cody Powell, Carson Wyatt, and I do not do these things every day, but we could, and no one would say a thing.

We are the opposite ends of the rainbow: totally different and exactly alike.

Stay the Course

We need somewhere to go,
  Some difference to make,
So we do not just wait,
  But must, rather, take
The helm and steer with a stronger eye.

We cannot claim to know,
  Even touched by grace,
If we seek with hopeless faith,
  Or may kiss the face of God
 In a sky of timeless stars.

For me, the course is clear,
  I do what needs to be done,
With no other thoughts
  Than defying the sun,
And to live with my hands on the wheel.

Part Two:
Ten Things Your Children Should Know after Graduation

Number One: Family and Friends

Family:

At your age, it is not uncommon to be trying to become independent, to move away from your family. But, over the next few years, your parents will begin to seem a lot smarter than they do now, and you will come to understand that your family is your only safe haven, your only real protection in a challenging and dangerous world.

You should thank them today for the love and support that helped you get this far. You worked hard, for sure, but so did they, and they deserve your gratitude.

Friends:

We all like to think of ourselves as friendly. Most of us have a lot of acquaintances and are socially active. However, when we need honest advice or loyal support in a crisis, we will be lucky if we have one or two friends we can count on to be there.

You should cherish these people and, as Shakespeare makes clear in *Hamlet*, "grapple them to thy soul with hoops of steel."

One of the best things I have done in recent years is to search out my old college buddy, who was also the best man at my wedding. The years just melted away. We are both sorry we lost track of one another, but we are both also glad that it wasn't too late.

Don't tempt fate. Keep in touch with good friends all the time.

Number Two: Sense of Humor

It is one thing to smile when it is sunny; it is quite another to sing in the rain. Humor will do at least two things for you:

It will keep you from taking yourself too seriously.

It will soften the heavy blows of life.

Abraham Lincoln was famous for telling lighthearted stories and poking fun at himself during our greatest national tragedy, the Civil War. When a friend commented that he could lose a second term if General Grant captured Richmond and was nominated as an opposing candidate, Lincoln reportedly replied, "Well, I feel very much about that as the man felt who said he didn't want to die particularly, but if he had got to die, that was precisely the disease he would like to die of."

Speaking of disease, people who laugh a lot are not only happier, but also may be healthier. Norman Cousins was the editor of a famous literary magazine. When he was hospitalized with cancer, he adopted a routine of watching classic comedies day after day. The doctors confirmed that his recovery to full health was aided by his determination to laugh the illness away.

Number Three: Work

Mark Twain once said, "Work and play are words used to describe the same activity under differing conditions."

You don't need to know what you want to do with the rest of your life right now, but you should be looking for it. Work can either be something you do because you need a paycheck, or it can be something you do because you love doing it. University studies indicate that your generation may change jobs five or six times. If you find your passion, throw yourself into it, learn every aspect of it, do all the unpopular parts that no one else wants to do, never watch the clock, and always strive for perfection.

You will spend more than half your life doing something. Whatever it is, or whatever series of things it is, you will be happier if you do it well.

Number Four: Money

Money isn't everything, but you do have to pay attention to it. This country lives on credit, and your generation is likely to continue that habit. Americans tend to spend money they haven't earned and to buy things they don't really need.

As we have all discovered recently, the bills eventually come due. With character and discipline, you can manage your finances wisely and prepare for your future.

Three thoughts:

Brendan Frasier once said, "People with money may be frustrated, unhappy, and depressed … but one thing is … they aren't broke."

The writer Sean Casey penned that "Money may not make you happy, but it quiets the nerves."

My son had an economics teacher who constantly repeated this advice: "Save, *dummkopf*, save!"

Number Five: Flexibility

Having core values is important. Being honest, loyal, and trustworthy are all great qualities. But beyond those things, the most successful people are open to new ideas and creative in their thinking.

One small personal example: When we were trying to build a new gymnasium at the Gow School, the local planning board took the summer off and could not hear our appeal of an earlier ruling that the gym could not be built because there was a flood plain on an isolated area of the more than one hundred–acre campus. Because of double-digit inflation at the time, the three-month delay would vastly increase the cost of the project. I went to the school attorney and had him create Gow School A and B. Gow School B was one acre and did not have a flood plain. The planning director issued a building permit the next day.

More significantly: Do you ever use the Internet? The guys who started Google were working on a term project. They now have the greatest search engine in the world and have become part of our language. We no longer look something up. We Google it.

Number Six: Take Calculated Risks

Once you get a good job and begin to save some money, there is the danger of "playing it safe." You may get into an emotional and financial rut that stunts your growth and keeps you from progressing as a person and a professional.

Without throwing away your gains, you may need to take a chance on something new. A different job or a different location may allow you to become a stronger human being.

I am not suggesting this as a way of giving yourself an excuse to run away from your responsibilities, but as a reminder that you can't always use your responsibilities as an excuse to avoid moving forward in your life.

I have had some good friends and colleagues who stayed in one place because it was home and their families were close to them, and in most of those cases, I believe they did the right thing. I have known just as many people who stayed put out of fear and insecurity.

Three times in my career, I accepted a new position in a different region of the country at a lower salary with greater obligations and more potential for leadership and growth.

At the same time, I was able to put down roots for almost fifteen years in each of my last two tours of duty. I made up the financial difference within two years in every case, and each job was better and more satisfying than the one preceding it.

When Roy Rogers, King of the Cowboys, began to make a weekly TV series, the producers offered only half his regular salary. Rather than turn it down, he asked for ownership of his professional name. They said okay, and it wasn't long before Roy was pulling in more than a million dollars from the sales of hats, cap guns, and lunchboxes to kids all over the world.

Number Seven: Diet and Exercise

It has taken me many years to deal properly with this concept. There were phases of my life in which I could be described accurately as a basketball with eyes.

My wife, Georgann, finally made me understand that bacon is not a major food group and that watching football does not qualify as a sport.

I think the key for your generation is balance and moderation. That is true if you are on the heavy side or if you are deliberately too thin.

Some people need therapeutic support to live a healthy life, but for most of us, it is a matter of common sense. You don't have to give up your guilty pleasures altogether … you can still visit In-N-Out … but you will feel better, diminish the chances of diabetes, reduce heart disease, and avoid an early stroke by being more aware and more consistent in your approach to food and if you also get sensible and moderate exercise.

Number Eight: Interests

You should have at least one interest outside of work that gives you pleasure and provides a break from the pressure of the office or providing properly for your family. This can be a physical or intellectual activity. Just remember, it isn't supposed to dominate. It is meant to supplement and nourish your life.

Norm Severe and Ernie Hartt are members of the staff at the Winston School. Norm escapes the stress of being a full-time counselor by driving his ATV in the desert on weekends, and Ernie gets a respite from the hectic pace of the computer center by participating in hot air balloon races.

My son collects vintage Volvos from the sixties and seventies. He searches out original parts from all over the world. We are determined to completely restore at least one of these revered classics.

My own hobbies have included making walking sticks from branches found at historical sites, learning to ride horses and jump fences, becoming a decent lawn bowler, and continuing to enjoy a reputation as an optimistic golfer.

Number Nine: Community Spirit

You need to get outside yourself and give something back to the community that has given you the opportunity to thrive. Whether you sell Girl Scout cookies, coach little league, build houses for the homeless, or help make New Orleans a great city again doesn't really matter. The important thing is to do the most you can do to improve the lives of other people and, therefore, improve your own as well.

In my retirement, I have been the Chairman of the Regional Planning Commission and continue to serve on five boards. None of these positions have produced any income. All have given me a great deal of satisfaction.

Number Ten: Issues

You are living in one of the most exciting periods in human history. The challenges and rewards ahead of you are highly significant and very much worth the effort.

Please don't waste time blaming your parents or the older generation for what ails the world right now. We had the same problem. No one has ever asked to be given a planet at risk. Our record isn't perfect, but we did a pretty good job:

We helped to end legalized segregation and participated in the civil rights movement, which continues to this day.

We advanced the rights of women to where more females are in college than males.

We took down the Berlin Wall and ended the nuclear cold war with Russia.

We put a man on the moon and satellites in space that allow us to talk to almost anyone anytime, anywhere, and watch more than 500 TV channels.

We achieved medical breakthroughs that have turned previously unthinkable operations into almost routine procedures.

If you do your job as well, by the time you retire, these things may also be true:

The average person will live more than a hundred years.

Automobiles will run on something simple and get eighty miles per gallon.

Terrorism will be eliminated by creative political cooperation between developed countries.

The Arctic won't melt, and there will be snow again on Mt. Kilimanjaro.

Women will routinely be elected President.

AIDS will be a distant memory.

No one anywhere will go hungry.

You have the talent and intelligence to become what Tom Brokaw called our parents: The Greatest Generation.

Don't shrink from this challenge. Do what Americans have always done and embrace it. We did our best for you. Now we are passing the torch and counting on you to make the world a better, safer, happier, and healthier place.

As you begin this great adventure, allow me to offer for sustenance along the way a few final words from men whose minds were far superior to my own:

The earth belongs to the living.

   —Thomas Jefferson

The … people for me are the mad ones, the ones who are mad to live, mad to talk, mad to be saved, desirous of everything at the same time, the ones who never yawn … but burn, burn, burn like fabulous yellow roman candles exploding … across the stars.

   —Jack Kerouac

Each morning when I open my eyes I say to myself: I have the power to make me happy or unhappy today. I can choose which it shall be. Yesterday is dead, tomorrow hasn't arrived yet. I have just one day, today, and I'm going to be happy in it.

   —Groucho Marx

When the crazy side roads beguile you, my son, take a long backward look at Monticello.

   —William Styron

That which we are, we are … one equal temper of heroic hearts … made weak by time and fate, but strong in will to strive, to seek, to find, and not to yield.

   —Alfred Lord Tennyson

Epilogue

I.

As you may have observed, this effort at poetry and prose is imperfect, but at least it is mine at my absolute imperfect best … and while it may imperfectly convey my thoughts as a minor contribution to our language and literature, it lets my grandchildren know that I was never afraid to try something new, that I always did the most I could with the imperfect gifts I was given, and that I hope they will do the same.

If they do, then that will be … just perfect

II.

I am not planning on having a tombstone, but perhaps my little box of ashes could bear the kind words of Carolyn Chandler, a former classmate who, after visiting with me for the first time in nearly fifty years, remarked:

We always thought of you

As solid and steady,

With a poet's heart.

Nothing has changed.

Acknowledgments

While I take full responsibility for any lack of quality and all errors, there are many people whose support made it possible for me to produce the book at all.

Dan Peragine is the art teacher at the Winston School. He created the cover design and supervised the included student work. Dan is an accomplished artist whose works in various media are appreciated all over the country. Not surprisingly, he was a member of the panel issuing grants in art education for The National Endowment of the Arts in Washington DC this year.

Nolan Inouye is a junior at Winston who drew the pieces for *Big Red; Billy, Doc and Wyatt; When Did I Become Irrelevant?* and *For David*. Nolan is interested in completing a Bachelor of Fine Arts degree after graduation.

Stefani Holland is also a junior. She drew the pictures for *Lorraine* and *Up with ABBA*. Stephanie looks forward to an education that will prepare her for a career in illustration or writing.

The staff and faculty at both Winston and the Gow School consist of dedicated professionals whose friendship made me a better teacher, a better leader, and a better person. A special note of gratitude goes to the late and lovely Judith Trethewey McCabe, David and Alice Gow, Dan and Jody Kelly, Paul and Kathy Rose, Todd and Sandra Avis, Bill and Nancy Adams, Mary Sterling-Torretti, Mindy Kaplan, Arnold Kairdolf, Andrea Goodman, the late John Richards, Mike and Ko Roston, John and Meredith French, and especially Louise Ukleja and Brent and Sarita Eastman.

Along with Ange Fatta, my friend and fellow movie critic for many years, my brother John and his wife, Ilene, helped me think carefully and make significant decisions on a number of occasions throughout my career. I am also very thankful that my old friends Lindalee Nielsen, Carolyn Chandler, Doug Cooper, John Parker, and Richard and Sandra Niederhauser, who gave me confidence in high school and college, are part of my life again.

No expression of appreciation would be complete without mentioning Dean Palmer, the inspirational Headmaster at the Overlake School in Redmond, WA, who, before passing away much too soon, gave me my first opportunity to learn and grow as a teacher and administrator.

The editorial evaluators, copy editors, and design staff at iUniverse are rigorous and thoroughly professional. I am especially grateful to Amy McHargue and Sarah Disbrow for their encouragement and support.

Most significantly, my son, Jason, read the manuscript and made insightful suggestions, while his wife, Kelli, walked me through a maze of technical issues. And as I neared the end of the final revisions of the book, my sister-in-law, Carol Kramer made an overly complex procedure seem almost routine.

Finally, nothing would ever have been written without the enduring love of my wife, Georgann, who also moved the publication date up about two years by relieving me of all typing duties.